WITHDRAWN

Chances are Few

To Bob
with all best wishes,
toward a better world

[signature]

LIBRARY
H.S. PERF. & VIS.
ARTS

Lorenzo Thomas

 Blue Wind Press Berkeley 1979

Copyright © 1972, 1975, 1977, 1979 by Lorenzo Thomas.
All rights reserved. No part of this book may be reproduced by any means, including information storage & retrieval or photocopying equipment, except for short excerpts quoted in critical articles, without written permission from Blue Wind Press.

Some of these works have previously appeared in *Attaboy, Big Sky, Chicago, The Human Handkerchief, A Hundred Posters, La-Bas, Milk Quarterly, New Black Voices* (New American Library), *Partisan Review, The Sun, Sunsprout, Telephone, United Artists, Vibration, The World, Y'Bird,* and *ZZZ*. Grateful acknowledgement is extended to the editors of these periodicals and anthologies.

LIBRARY OF CONGRESS CATALOGING IN PUBLICATION DATA:
Thomas, Lorenzo, 1944—
    Chances are few.

    I. Title.
PS3570.H568C5   811'.5'4   79-18968
ISBN 0-912652-57-8
ISBN 0-912652-56-X pbk.
ISBN 0-912652-58-6 signed/numbered cloth

This first edition was designed by George Mattingly; typeset in Cartier & Raleigh by Dave Mattingly and Robert Sibley; pasted up by Alan Bernheimer; and manufactured in Autumn 1979 for Blue Wind Press, Box 7175, Berkeley, California 94707.

The cover collage, "After the Fall," is copyright © 1979 by James Farber. Photo of the author by Betty Tichich, *Galveston Daily News*.

79 80 81 4 3 2 1

Contents

9   My office

THE FINE CLOTHES OF YEAR BEFORE LAST

15   Inauguration
16   The Fine Clothes of Year Before Last
18   Farting as Decency
19   Sugar Hill
20   Security
22   Personal Anthropology
24   Broadway-Lafayette Espadrille
29   Euchre Bridge
30   Wheeling
32   Too Loud for Names
33   The Rule of Thumb

THEY NEVER LOSE

44   The Leopard
46   They Never Lose
52   Too Much One Thing, Not Enough Somewhat Else
55   Choosing Metals
56   Guilt
57   Canzone
58   Sketches of Susan
61   Electricity of Blossoms
63   Hiccups *after Leon Damas*
68   Instructions for Your New Osiris
70   Shake Hands with Your Bets, Friend

THE MARVELOUS LAND OF INDEFINITIONS

- 78 The Marvelous Land of Indefinitions *after Roberto MacKay*
- 82 When Dukardo Boarded the Astro-Jet, He Already Done Seen the Movie *after Dukardo Hinestrosa*
- 84 Home X XI
- 85 MMDCCXIII
- 86 *an excerpt from* Big House Movies
- 90 Screen Test
- 101 Class Action
- 112 Hat Red
- 116 Clear Channel

for D

My Office

I've spent the last 10 years
In other people's offices
Learning the alphabet of nods and eyebrows
And pursed lips, straining for the purse
Legs crossed in easy confidence
Confident nervous gestures of assurance
Approved blue suits
And sudden dreamed-up lies to be delivered

A net of thirty days and sixty days and ninety
Insanely stretched past promise into years
Next week, for certain
Floated haphazardly on possibles
As slight as handshakes,
Firm as agreements of subjective verbs

And got nowhere.

This happy corner, sucking up hard-boiled eggs
And polish hots
The seidel sliding down the polished bar
Clatter of friendly pool balls in the margin
Not exactly somewhere, but a certain place.

A regular's dark hair and polished eyes
Glow in the glasses lined before her face
Smoking and berating the muzak
"Jack, when you gonna get some country music?"

"Country Charlie Pride?"

Outside, it's as bright as the important phone call
I always pretend to await
Setting up the lunch meeting at Stouffer's
Linen napkins and hope's frozen green peas

Set up another round of handshake laughter for the pictures

"Hey sweet thing, when we gonna have that date?"
The barmaid pouts a 1940s frown—
It's Arnie (reaching now to slap me on the back)
A gleaming brazen polyester clown,
Tuesday seems longer than the day before
Since I began to organize my life around My Office
I stay a little later every day.
A little rain hangs fire in the clouds

Next trip, I think I'll bring the wife

THE FINE CLOTHES OF YEAR BEFORE LAST

Lucas Cranach the Elder: *The Judgment of Paris,* 1530, Baden Art Museum, Karlsruhe, West Germany.

"They call me Sugar Daddy
I am the softest touch in town."
—*Mercy Dee*

Inauguration

The land was there before us
Was the land. Then things
Began happening fast. Because
The bombs us have always work
Sometimes it makes me think
God must be one of us. Because
Us has saved the world. Us gave it
A particular set of regulations
Based on 1) undisputable acumen.
2) carnivorous fortunes, delicately
Referred to here as "bull market"
And (of course) other irrational factors
Deadly smoke thick over the icecaps,
Our man in Saigon   Lima   Tokyo   etc   etc

The Fine Clothes of Year Before Last

Only fit now
For the garden, the carwash,
The ritual of stinking for four days
To solve a problem
That stinks to you to high heaven
And just in general stinks

Sweating and sleeping
In these shabby clothes
An almost Biblical humility

Remember the pretensions of these slacks
Outmoded now by cuffs
That once were fashionable
Now only blows to style's ego

The shirt's stiff vanity
Long ago frayed into a makeshift coverup
For Saturday mornings' inopportune doorbells
That scheme to steal the self-bestowed rewards
Of a week's toil and Friday night good fortune
A shirt so homely and contrite,
Those days were brave. The only peals
It dares to answer lately are the phone's.
Original function almost completely faded from memory
Superseded by last month's soft stars:
The sad blue one featuring Bette Midler's lips
The dashing gold with Mondrian motifs
Haughtily synthetic carefree exaggerations,
slouching on hangers,

These treasure their trips to the cleaners
Like sad husbands playing at wit in distant cities
Like old fools with young girls anywhere at all
While old stud gets funky
And goes straight through the wringer
With rags, dirty drawers and soiled linen.
One with experience,
No novelties or mysteries remain ahead.
No mystique remaining.
So agitated and spun by lifelong turnings, even the bones
Would be lost long ago if they weren't stitched in.

This shirt feels softer than the world it once confronted,
Suitable now only for faceless moods
    That's the necessity that summons all
Things
    The only reason they are still around
Perhaps

    That
Someday
    They shall be useful beyond purpose

The matching tie, though, is still splendid
Still wide in vogue
Living in the glove compartment
An emergency cravat.
It has folded itself into this honor
Its true office diminished
By the fate of its shirt

Farting as Decency
à John Berryman

Someone essays the ultimate step
Which illuminated the late news
And gives us something odd to relate
To the next afternoon at the Club.

When *you* die, of course, you will abhor
Any reference to yourself over a beer
Or tom collins. You will appreciate any
Respite in a drunkard's consideration

Of you and your first wife. Your departing
This life of toil, manners and strife.
You'll appreciate any skip in the record
Of your descent. The bar maid's fart.

Sugar Hill

How you like that?

Quadrasonic baby

When you turn these speakers up
Behind this music
A breeze actually blows
Through the room. Man!

That's how come I believe engineers
Truly exist

Though we cannot see them

Security

> No headaches or heartaches
> Or misunderstands . . .
> —*Thomas A. Dorsey*

All Americans are losing
Their minds are going crazy
With the fear of being
Alone
In the world
Going nowhere

The air marshals of the future
Search everyone at the gate

> Americans must go nowhere
> —THE DIRECTOR

On the bulletin board

This is undisguised information
Nothing covert no leaks no culvert
& no Calvert

I declare!

The speaker
Announced no changes of seaport
The move is to be made by air

No charts. Somehow they'll get there
That's what all the bon voyageurs share
That simple hope waving their hankies

All Americans are going going
"Those honkies!" hissed
The protestants at the pier

And "I, too, am an American"
Dreamed a lovely desirable gone white girl
Marvelously sedated in a chair

Personal Anthropology

How abject beauty are
Our own reflections
They show so little of us

Our syllables dwindle in this beauty
Like colors in shadows of turrets
Walls
Selfish determinations
As we transfer our pain
To a Monet a pattern of colors
Seurat and pointed lines

In our small rooms in fronds of TV sets
We become pointillistes of conversation

Our own problems grow
No larger
As we quietly sit
Amused by the fun
Watching several deranged little people
Tormented in a box on the table

Total boredom's majesty
We forge a newer Milarepa   learning

Suffering proudly and silent
Bravely at bedtime
Absorbing the shocks
Of the news. Sadnesses
And policies doomed

At last, compassion for a President
Poor Gerald Ford

Broadway-Lafayette Espadrille

DIARY OF A SOLDIER

6th Avenue. 28th Street.
The green bus appeared
Headed uptown. Determined.

Full of rabbis with earlocks
And beards. Backwardly
Thumbing their books
Past the towering greed
Each deliberate corner
Halting their speed
Toward a promised appearance
Somewhere uptown I guess

POPULAR FORCES

Hum, said a beautiful sister
Glad I'm not a Jew

WRONG FACE HUH

I think I understand how she felt
Not really understanding I guess
Grown men with beards on the shule bus
Collecting ignorant comments
Imperturbably headed uptown

But then, what could you tell her?
Count neckties in the Subway?

BRIEFING

The ignorance of appearance
Holding everyone back
Or the ignorant traffic

THE RIGHT FACE

Bring

I hear the second alarm. I leap and
Shrug on my sneakers and dash
To the front of the shape up
Prepared check ready check do it
Check. I load my Malcolm X book
In my back pocket for lunchtime

A MESSENGER (MY SLAVE)

A good job. I go sweeping through
The City machinegunning the buildings
My eyeballs red from so many
Rounds. With my satchel under my arm
Walking into the lobbies and freight
Doors in the immaculate fronts
Of the City's tawdry business
And the words coded between each
End of a luncheonette counter

CONTACT REPORT

Too much reefer this morning. Too much wine last night?

FORWARD

The Broadway number jumbled up in my brain
My mind's dream of Walt Frazier
And/or Black Revolution. And *rifa*
All down to my feet moving swift

In my sneakers. Is this the wrong Broadway?

Swoop back downtown. The same burthen
Too much reefer
On my head back and forward
Through the City all day

THROUGH THE NEEDLE'S EYE

Carrying Seventh Avenue dresses
Packages of careless fortune
For the Man for the ignorant
Beautiful sisters buying
This garbage sale day
At Ohrbach's for nearsighted Jews
And yenta daughters in law
From Lake Success and Ft Lee
New Jersey. Back downtown down
Through Hell's Half-Acre back
Now to Broadway and Lafayette
And its alarming psycho-sexual
Capitalist charm

PRESENT ARMS

Long silken hair big leg Puerto Rican ladies of sensuous
Armpits.

Rap to this one
Hey *¡corazon!*
I got *azucar pa ti*
Dig? *Me el mensajero*
You dig? She frown
And is gone down
The busy street and
I wonder what it is
Or where it is

And I wonder just where
In Hell I am. Dammit,

I'm lost

ATTENTION

A white woman with flat feet
Looks out of her window
She looks oddly at me off
The rim of her eyeglasses

My Malcolm X book in my pocket

Eyes slitted standing here lost like a fool
On the most businesslike wrong corner
In the currency world of our days. Man.

I'm attracting all this attention?

PARADE REST

A bundle of dresses with no woman smell yet
On my head

My two dreaming feet
On the ground

Euchre Bridge

> Allow the prophets to hold the Eucharist as they will
> —*Didache, 10:7*

Grateful,
I sit and watch
This yellow butterfly
Dip into Chinese tallow

I watched the lowest leaves
Turn orange and then red

They vanished then
Too stylish for the tree

Went off to the city & lights

Now there's about a dozen red leaves
                                    higher up
A yellow butterfly plays
All around them, tempted

Goes off in search of true flowers
Dummy!
     At this late date
It gets early
        darker than it used to

Poor butterfly

Wheeling
for Clement & Lewis

So

That's redneck music man just wait
You awake just in time
To see the next exit
And remark similar signs

You have seen somewhere
Before. This awakens
The driver and evoked

Gratitude from the death seat
Where I been riding
Alone with the bland view
Of the landscape of that
Highway so like any other
And so dull

That is, lacking the remarks of the roadmaps
Annotating and expanding
As our landmark
The beautiful mountains add
Defiance or yearning
To the depressed States

As the highway captures our car
Which makes no distinctions
Between mountains and States

That is rightly the work of the maps
Pimping the restrooms we desire

Hush your mouth

Just wake up & yr mouth already!
Welcome back to God's country
Wait. I'm *trying* to find the soul
Plus the tape died

About twenty miles down the road

The batteries couldn't stand
All that ignorance in the air
Plus you were asleep
All the way from Ohio

Get yourself together brother man

Nearing home now. You wake up just in time
Take the wheel

Too Loud for Names

She becomes a sagging bosom
Big behind   "movin in
Forty-one years of her
         movin out
Voluptuous & fine
         disco lady . . ."
As beautiful as she has been she is
         Black and
Fading fast   lovely
Before your greedy eyes
         and shy.

She becomes an academic question
When the band wraps up
         no rendezvous
Saying "Take care y'hear
         no voulez vous
We'll be right here back again
         no "me & you"
         tonight
This coming Thursday. All right!"
At home, the sitter watches Johnny Carson
The kids are wrapped up tight.
Yes, momma loves *them*.

The Rule of Thumb
for Ron Padgett

I

Opening a can of Coors
In Tulsa, beneath a full moon
Near the Sun Oil refinery
East of Sun Oil west of the moon
Press press and push, thumb ending
Up in the beer
Shake thumb and lick
Sip

Kinda warm (don't you think)
Stand lookout by the window
All clear sneak to ice machine
I-legal bucket held rushing style

Trip

Run back and rebound
Slide back to room along the Trail of Ice
Slip

Back into the room (careful) and ice the Coors
Make two more forays.

Have used up now nine people's share
But, then, there're 60 vacant rooms here.
Tonight's only Monday
An off day in the motel game
Just like in the life,

Blue Monday Blue Monday
But no heart-rending music
No "Rocks In My Bed"
No call me the Winding Boy Everybody Know
My Name
You know you know you know
You know my name
Look up, the number's
On the bottom of the can

No

Torchy songs sputter down
Smooth as faded denim
Muzak
Annoying ooze into the lobby
As very few people check in.
And even fewer fumble
For American Express cards

And there is none
To remark the clerk's boredom
Just an off day in the motel game
In Tulsa

On edge on the outskirts of town,
Those few behind doors,
Whose windows glow,
Are watching Melissa Manchester
Once again flunk the Memorex test
Wishing they had instead
Gone to Europe for the Silver Jubilee
To buy a cup with the Queen's mug

Upon it (GUARANTEED UNBREAKABLE
MARCIA REGISTRADA
NOT AUTHORIZED FOR RADIO BROADCAST)
Touch and go
Hecho en Mexico
Cop and blow
Recycled from obsolete Don Ellis records
b/w *Electric Mexicana Rose*
That, in those days, were "ahead
of their time"—*Billboard*
36⅓ on the A side, 46 rpm
On the flip
Gone to Jackson
Jackson Jacksonville
Bowling Green
Or New Orleans

Gone on to New Orleans
To see the mystic treasures of King Thumb,
Sarcophagus mask hammered of Coors
Cans recycled by superstitious fellahin

In the good old days before Palestinians
Were content to pose with their asses
For roving color photographers
Who, with Christian charity and Hasselblads
Immortalized those ingrates in child Bibles
Ennobling skyjacking heathen souls with captions:
These are, perhaps, the scenes that Jesus saw

Ah, sands of time!
Tan snows of yesteryear!
Deserts of memory shift in our minds

Drip
Through the bottle of the picture tube
Cyrus Vance
Kissinger
When they begin the beguine
As electrons
Under Tulsa's fool moon
In this motel's one room
I'm sitting in, watching TV
Escaped from the frayed Blues in the lobby
Muzak
My mind reminds me
Texarkana and Alphonso Trent
Was Music those days

My mood
Reminds me
Of Ron's "Radio"
Tulsa
1921
The riots "riots"
Instead of the Jazz Age
T for Tulsa
T for Tennessee
Bob Wills for Texas
San Antonio Rose
And all that and
Vo de oh doh

Voodoo   Class of '21

Instead, niggers screaming
No jazz

Houses burning
No shimmy
And T too many white folks dreaming
Freak dreams that could never be.
Ignorance churning
These disasters into the brew
That flows out of the mountains
Where the Arkansas rises
Now, under this moon
As you press press and push
Cut your thumb
On the lip of the press-tab
Opening the swirling seals of King Thumb
Mystic treasures of ancient waltz music

Here's your INSTRUCTIONS:
Cut thumb and suck
You are blood brother now

Blood, brother

Ah ee ah hah
Are these the scenes what Jesus saw
With color prints of Colorado's valley
And chicano workers walking picket lines
Is this what Carter and Carnarvon saw
In cursed relics now touring the land
In Ronald Reagan's real DEATH VALLEY DAYS
Press press and push and millions for that cause
More where that came from
And millions flocking everywhere to view
In New Orleans King Thumb and in Chicago

Uh huh ah yeah
You are blood brother now
To weighted hatreds
Of all the centuries
All the enormities of recent years

Of Coors

II

PURIFY   PURIFY   PURIFY

Howling a chant to the full moon in Tulsa,
I see the guests stick their heads out their doors
They gleam in the full moon of Tulsa

The faded Blues unravels in the lobby
An off day in the motel game
The night clerk simply snores

I see a shadow in the moon: Our time is hard
It's hard. But fair. And it is just.

Just T for Tulsa
T for Tennessee
T for you too, brother by me

As the spirits are rising
In the light of the moon
Drink *Miller's* (though it's 30¢ more)

We must cling to our vices to prove we are real
But we must also concern ourselves with the main deal

If you're fat, be forgiven
Drink *Lite*

Drink *Schlitz, Anheuser-Busch, Oly
Dos Equis,* even *Stag* near beer
But first of all
Of all the things to do in Tulsa,

BOYCOTT COORS

THEY NEVER LOSE

Claude Rains in *The Invisible Man*,
Universal Pictures, 1933, reprinted by permission.

No one
has ever
given me
an even break
but God

—*Percy Mayfield*

The Leopard

The eyeballs on her behind are like fire
Leaping and annoying
The space they just passed
Just like fire would do

The ground have no mouth to complain
And the girl is not braver herself

She is beautiful in her spotted
Leopard ensemble. Heartless so

To keep her fashionable in New York
Leopards are dying

Crude comments flutter around her
At lunchtime. She sure look good
She remembers nine banishing speeches

More powerful than this is the seam
Of the leotard under her clothing

Her tail in the leotard is never still
The seam!
She feels it too familiar on her leg
As some crumb says something suggestive

The leopard embracing around her
Is too chic to leap and strike

Her thoughts fall back to last semester's *karate*

Underneath, the leotard crouches up on her thigh
It is waiting for its terrible moment!

They Never Lose
after Cranach

A woman's sense is not her education
But what escapes from Logic,
Literature, and fads of aim
For security's sake, "set your cap for a doctor"
A dentist. At least, a real estate man.

So girls go daft
With or without education
Thinking up men as special Bargain prizes
That only need a little polishing,

A little work. So, they get married
Then, to sanctify the fact, they must buy *something*.
Whatever. A major purchase.
In the final showroom, tired of dallying,
"Jew him down" floods to her mind
In half-whispers. Theatrical for days.

You go for that?

Well, Rubens ate it up

Thought he was smart, too
Meddling mythology. I tried to tell him
Cranach tried to complain
About the silly hat, but who
Can tell a real or would-be goddess?

Chattlesome morons call it "human nature"
Popping their eyes at any lisp of news.

But, then again, what else is human nature?

Yeah?
How about him, who sees his dreams
Feel too large for the golden ring
A woman with or without education
Sees him performing in?
His purse knows better even if his heart
Is pumping bleeds of Red Grooms
Lithographs from the spring
Trip to New York City. For the foyer.

II

Take this badge off of me
I can't use it anymore.
It's getting dark,
Too dark to see;
I feel like I'm knocking on Heaven's door
—*Bob Dylan*

He sees himself an exile in his flesh
Flitting from place to place to relocate
And earn promotions. Finally to some nondescript Chicago,
An overdone but prim Lake Forest home,
Working till nine to pay the premium on his estate.

Be careful, daughter . . .

When the everyday commuter's
Train of thought
Stops short approaching minute stations
Along the pilgrimage to or from toil
And modest dreams of freedom

Ranking somewhere below wealth
But near to comfort
Where no known drug's peace
Is more inebriating
Than the tiresome but firmly-held belief
That pain will vanish in the afternoon,
When thought and music masters noise
As effortless as you please,
Umm hmmm. That's when it crashes!

*

OK, I'd classify that one as a dream
—or a disaster.

Lucky we live down South
Everything is flat around here
Even, they tell me, our pronunciation.
That's why we use these big words
Our betters and the redskins left behind

I mean, like "nigra," "pickaninny," "Tennessee"

*

Just then, it happens.
The boss (who never liked this dude)
Begins to wonder
"Say Jim, you think
You might could handle
Nashville?"

Unseemly pride of Equal Opportunity
The presidency of the local NAACP
Fades into visions of the local Klan
Clumsily setting up a sputtering rood

On your front lawn in Nashville, Tennessee:
That's what you get for your mouth
Saying you love her more than life itself

III

The there it is,
I swear to God

That's when it happens:
Dimly, he wavers
Like tv sets of those too cheap to subscribe to the cable
Who can't afford it because their lives are sad
Because there is some tragedy way back
That kept them pure and poor in quarantines of sense

Quite educational.

That's when he wakes metabolized in sleep
Without her cool, soft hand to soothe his sweat
After the dream that shows in twenty years
His broken body managing the shop in South Dakota

Or, worse than that, consulting in New York
Dodging muggers, while she sits watching *Kojak* in Tulsa
As he frets sitting, lonely in an Oyster Bar
Of some dull town's insipid Marriott
Watching ugly blond waitresses bore him
Finally to the disgraceful confession:

"I've made a complete omelette of my life!"

Or else
She sits complacent in her negligee
Watching soap operas

Chewing and snapping gum to old time movies
Dinah Shore
The $100,000 waste of time
While he swinks on at luncheons, demonstrations,
Conferences, sales meetings, briefings, and arguments,
She sits

Becoming sunlight flatters her awhile
While simple sense tells him that women age
Longer than men, since men have heart attacks
From overwork. And, dammit, he can see it all now!
A sense of time or timing counsels him,
Beware. Women have tricks up their sleeves
Even naked

So, sensible women always understand,
A young man's pride goes on the punctual shelf
Of duty after the first date
Until the crucial moment when he dreams
Again of flirting with himself in his disguises:
Always clean and cool
Single, and, for that reason,
Free to act a fool.

IV

Helen dramatized the smallest incidents . . .
—*Anais Nin*

Only a foolish child falls to despair.

At this point, woman reaps
The fruit of sisterhood.
People will talk. It does her good to listen

Even if they heap badmouth on her man,
It's good advice, experience, instructions.
You want an apple or a wedding ring?

Paris my foot. The thought! That stuck-up
Sucker

One man, three women
Who he think he is?

One who thinks she's got him
    Even if he strays
One who yearns to keep him
    If he stays
One who feels she's lost him
Still dreams of other days
My dear, it's worth your time to learn
At least those three graces,
And not be caught confused
Between a man's natural two-facedness

Lord, yes! A woman's strength

That leaves
Him, who fears another's feeling,
Defeated finally in merely choosing
Defeated formally in memory's anticipations
Like the last time you thought you saw
Just what you thought you saw
A kind of fleeting shame and frozen sorrow;
Control of nothing left but needless options

But now, the deal was closing in her eyes

Too Much One Thing, Not Enough Somewhat Else
Progressive Reggae

O brother stay strongest

None but a no good woman tries to fool you
A good one understands it's not her place to rule
You, as equals share
You know what sharing's like:
She'll wake up coughing
In the middle of the night
And ask if *you're* all right

Stay strongest, brother.

Not even necessary to shed a tear;
Just the unstable moisture of confusion only
Condensing
Trembling a strong voice
To catch or whimper
Is enough . . .
The first drop of the torrent and the flood
Not after ever to be denied
(Weakness in a man, brother)
Neither by myth, plain lie,
Historical necessity nor convoluted
Faith

No faith camouflage for weakness
Weathered board and even dumb stone speaks
Even to the most unsophisticated sensors
The high water mark is evidence enough

Visible in your structure of relations

The line that remains gauges weakness
Inadequate plans
Endurance perhaps, like a campaign scar
But strength is not the same thing as endurance
Which speaks to weakness first in private,
Confidently carrying its pleas to higher courts
As the flood rises where the rich folks live.

Each house its own nilometer,
The high water mark is what speaks
Relief for survival, not pride;
Thankfulness for endurance, not praise
Testament to struggle and shameful evidence of weaknesses
Covers every stone on the planet like grafitti
Darkly whistling boasts of terrified Senior Classes
Gone down the drain long ago.
The high water mark is etched in every rock
Humility of uncountable forgotten Pharoahs

Monuments to the weakness of man.

Embarrassment
A bathtub ring coloring our new mutual cleanliness
Trust that!
Experience too clear to be denied
Floating about us, granulated
Dead moons of Saturn
Gleaming and telling. Oh brother!

No one, please,
Mishear me. No one
Must take their pleasure in offense

Of what I say to tell my brother
Brother, always stay strongest.
Unless the lamb must be called chauvinist
To fear the shepherd's pie,
This is just an old ram's bleating

Brother, stay strongest always

For even once you fight away the fever
Which comes like a gift with freight charges,
No strength of protest,
Strategy, disgust, or plan . . .
No plea ever will move
The soft cooling weight of her hand
Loving,
Concerned until governing,
From your brow

You don't need consultations with gypsies,
Bump-readers, or the Corps of Engineers
You just look for the high water sign and the old folks
They will tell you about it
As old Joseph did learn to tell dreams
And the scales at the grain elevator:
Too much one thing, too little somewhat else.

The lines across an old man's forehead
Are lines from a young woman's hand
Imprinted there. It's only natural

She herself old, her palm shines (giving, golden, open)
Smooth as glass.

Choosing Metals

This child and the Moon are not speaking.

She has no use for it
If it's not silver. She
Prefers sleep to sunshine.
Her choice of metals
Is a natural

She prefers silver to presents

Her wristwatch and the key are gold-
Colored. She dares not use them

The child never wants milk
On her jello. She cries,
This is too precious for just dessert!

But really it's nothing

Guilt

No longer the feather
She used
To be, her breath still sings

But her head on my pyjama sleeve
Is heavy with confused
Determination & vague hurt

My heart
A stone cast in a lake
Catching a sudden freeze
Prisoning the stone
    Half in half out

Rings
Of ice which won't melt

    The rarity of what we've felt
Seems done

In the morning's radiance
When we wake,
She's unsure of my silence
As she chats about the weather

But all I want to talk about
Would be unspeakable things

Canzone

Strained daybreak breaks in past the blinds
You have your sexy moments with the sluts
And then the sensual response becomes a habit

Birds out of habit utter their sun spells.

Your habit strains
As her delusion finds
Your way to bland
Disgraceful petulances

Blocked. The tape feeds tacit
Arrogance to habit. Madnesses.
The radio announcer's pains
Of authenticity. We understand.

She walks out with Janis Joplin's CHEAP THRILLS

As local "music of the Renaissance" abuts
Her vocal memories of the Shirelles.
O Lord, how vain we are! Ghost music fills

Our Sundays with whatever is at hand
and Idries Shah's THE WISDOM OF THE IDIOTS

Sketches of Susan

She tilts her head
To hear the light
Which flows, like her hair
Billows
Turns around
Bob Dylan has it "Bette Davis-style"
Hands in
For your gaze's consideration
Hands in her pockets, tilting her head

Now you see her now you don't understand
What you see in her now
A fragment of a simple pose she wears
This one the girl from the plains
This one, the small town aesthete
Her heart in Venice for the Bienniale
A debutante refusing to come out.

Now you see her, here, touching a child with glee
And wonder that all Creation exists
Inside the child, inside her caring glance

And now suppose
That she pretends to be a pose a modern woman
Which is completely a shrug
That is, a shrug a long-stepped gait
& a turn (hands in pockets)

Bette Davis style

Mary Cassatt-style, studying the people at large

In their own moments
Painting their postures
But this one, this one who is not Cassatt,
Keeping their eyes to herself
Giving them ordinary representational eyes
Only because portraits have eyes
She gives them eyes, keeping all hope
All sorrow pretense pain all joy and wonder in those gazes
For herself
To still the postures
That those eyes dictate.

She herself poses. Everytime she paints.
And if I were a poet, I'd pose her in two words:
I'd make them up
I'd pose her   that way
And   that way, too

Lithe   gyroscopic

The self-portrait Mary Cassatt somehow just didn't paint

I'd pose her turning
Smiling at the sky
Shaking her hair inside a cotton field

Touching a child with wonder
Like a wand

Being a modern woman as she sees it
Which, really, she (like all of them)
Really don't see. Don't see that our lives
Are mere charades with constant wonder
And surprises we might have seen coming

And got the better of them

But I, like Frank O'Hara, am no painter.
And I fumble to offer no portrait,
Just sketches of Susan as sometimes I see her.
In two words, to show what a poor poet I am

Lithe, gyroscopic
Hearing light

Is there some old song that says it? some poem?
Some set of tones that paints a portrait in the light
In the way that light plunges through windows
Into the space of our poses . . . our bodies styled
In such light as if we were posing the one possible portrait
That impossibly tells all generations "So there!"
Hands in pockets, turning. That's who they were.

She's inside now inside
A room she's made a garden of
Her plants her space her portraits filled with love,
Moving like a diamond stylus
In the song of light which flows
Around & through her
From her hand
Returning to our eyes
The gift of what she sees
So well,
She tilts her head to hear

Portraits have eyes

Electricity of Blossoms
for Janet

Plentiful light

Their voices glow in mirror language
A high tension key winding
Brightness called "sky"
These things are atmospheric

Another electricity blossoms
The formal illusionist's hoop

Wireless

    Outside of the daylight
Inside,
  If one could be
  Outside of the light

    The light would appear
From within

Faith

I said, "Little brown electric flower/woman"

Convention

Lady your smile
A shock to my eyes

      An oriel in a tree

Your concern is the tree

                Your frown leaves

Plentiful light

Feelings are almost arabic in this poem

Levitation

My idea blossoms & varies like Light
Embracing light in the glass of a mirror.
A woman. Illusion of someone
Desiring magic tuxedos of mirrors

People who grow closer to surfacing

See stepping out of TG&Y or LEONARD'S

Closer to escaping into day
            trams

Hiccups
after Leon Damas

Seven gorgeous waters. Gulp!

Three or four times past twenty-four hours
I remember my childhood infancy
In a hiccup sequence

hiccup hiccup Pope pap hiccup hiccup

      instinct, man . . .

*

My mother gave her son good table manners

*

A fork is not a toothpick!
Don't talk with your mouth
Full of worldviews

When you lift your nose do it right!

Snap beans not salty equals pas sale

Zodico? By all means, no!

Kung Fu fighting no street friends no no
My daddy say let that boy boogie woogie
No no!

A typical West Indian childhood.

And then and then
The Father's name
Of the son

And the holy ghost
Ends in each grace
Fluttering above every meal

Grace to be born and transpired
In every variously memorable dinner pahty

Call it   grace
*

Shucks!
*

My mother, Mom
Taught her son memorandums
History lessons in a minor scale
        on the piano

    Church soup

Yesterday with the yesterday news
    History lessons:

Each child will bear the brunt
Of our Father's name

        Our Father . . .
*

You you take you
You can't even speak French!
French French
The real French French
French of France

Disaster

I tell myself disaster
Talking to me

My mom taught her son
My mother's son

      You have no future salutes
      from salesmen

      The ones you & I meet
      on the street

High or underground Savannah
in the shadow of the Dead's monument

    jazz   playing

In your "drum battle" with Otis,

             Otis
who hasn't even made a comeback
          from his
      baptism
Can't even speak French   dig it?

Disaster
I tell you disaster
I say to myself

*

My Ma
wanted a very do boy
ver-rey very me
very fa   no popping off fresh
   So
      very very

lah de dah, see?
        NO HOOKY PLAYING

I remember again it comes to me:
Your *violin* lessons!
A banjo
You say a banjo
How you say it
A banjo you say, "Good . . . a banjo"

HICCUP!!!

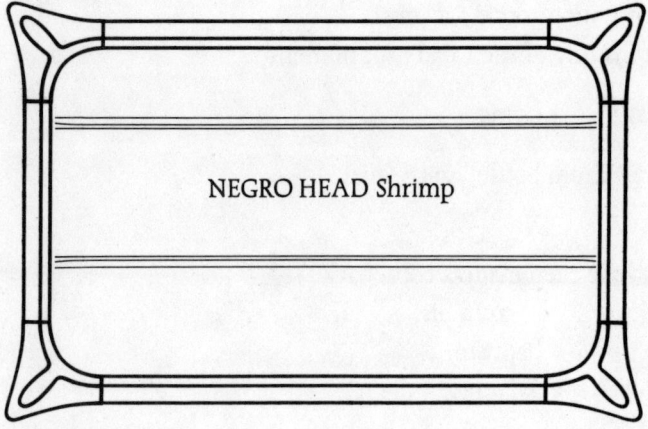

Such labels!

No sir
No siree
No ban
No "Joe"
No "git!"
No tears
No shit
No blues
No more

*
So

    There's no MULATTO water-fountain south of here . . .

So

    Let me drink the BLACK water!

Instructions for Your New Osiris

Canopic old Egyptian jugs,
The jars in her boudoir hold me.
Or used to
Since she's moved them
Put them in her bag
And toted them to her new lover's house

That's what she throws in my face
Since she no longer holds me
Since she can't stand to stay around
No longer

My heart's in one

I'm dead
        because no longer does my body hold a heart

Another holds what's left of pride
The day my best friend laughed dead in my face
Because he knew she was his other best friend's
Lady

Another holds the essence
Of my self-respect
And still another, all my tenderness
For her

That's all.
      There's nothing left
But dead politeness

Not even passion left to kick her ass

She lies progressively to me
Each day, like the difficulty
Of game show questions
A little bitter more ridiculous each time
And unbelievable

Where is Gene Rayburn? Adrienne Barbeau?
George Gobel? Wally Cox? Familiar faces of the afternoon
Clifton Davis? Margaret Daniels?
It seems I just don't understand this show.

Lying, she cheats

In front my face, behind my back
It doesn't matter
The only novelty is tonight's choice
A movie with my girlfriend
Got a date, I really didn't think you'd be in town
Don't hate me do you? Please
Don't hate me please
I'm sorry, but I didn't think you'd mind
Of how she wants to let me know
We're through

When I was still alive, before I knew
The full name of the door,
I used to speak of her and say
"My Lady"

Shake Hands with Your Bets, Friend

Every bookie
On the phone to Vegas
Odd
But all the trunk lines
Are tied up,
Sorry. This trunk is not seaworthy, sir.
In all good faith, I cannot
And other blasts from the past
No sir no good no sir
Such accents no longer seem strange;
Simply, they take their places
Next to the treasured linen in the trunk

Clean linen was prized so.

And silk, symbolic. Heraldry
Amid the horseshit; oriental mystery
Shining out imperial futures
Come a cropper in the knots of the dragon
Appliqued on the blouse
So carefully folded second down to the linen
And the silk tinted gold to go with the uniform serge
Of the master's desire for glory
Infecting all the crew with inertia
Obedience to the odds against survival
Cutting the Captain cutting
All of this loose, drifting free.

From the slaveship dock
Down dusty streets to auction block,

Awash in a chance for survival
No sir no good no sir
Until such accents no longer seem strange
He trudges

He drudges himself into choices before him
Using instincts and applied mathematical factors
The best advice is ask the winner
Bub, your guess as good as mine.

The choice is not acceptance nor adjustment
Nothing defiant definite at this time,
But give me a call in a day or two, he says;
From then on what? sack-cloth and cinders
Sandaled feet and a threatening sandwichman sign?

That's horseshit.
You either beat em or join em
Pays your money and you takes your choice
Everyone's a winner
EVERYONE'S A WINNER!
And other stale blasts from the past
No sir no good no sir
You'll be out there all by your lonesome!

Silks and silver fittings,
Your lonesome!

Riding free
To the roses, arched into the lucky horseshoe
A horticulturist piece against natural resistance
Circular winnings of really knowing the odds
Not even enjoying *A Day At The Races*
As it appears on late night tv yet again

At least the umpteenth time, but a respite
Of inexorable glee amid the usual horseshit

Resistance is natural, at first
Its lifeless monument
Suppression seems to rule
That's the usual horseshit

Show me a man

I sit here, for some reason, listing
Possibilities and ideas for packing a trunk
Or a kerchief
But leaving now is really going nowhere
New, not phrased or worried so bad
But confusing, that's what runs through
My mind concocting an elegant logic

Show me any slavery

A confusion of mail-order brides arrives
With careful trunks of hope and promises
Clutched in the letter packets in their hands
As dreams go sailing
Well damn how many *did* you send for sir
No sir no good no sir
You've got to choose

Off-track betting parlors are stormed!
Jostling
Throngs pushing and shoving
Thinking, soon he will choose.
Every bookie on
The phone to Vegas

People getting trampled down in the streets
In the mad rush to the window
As dated futures fling themselves
Into space from the top of office buildings
State capitols, from islands of pompous parkways
Skirting the miserable ghetto
They fling themselves on ignorant traffic
Short-tempered, sacrificial and vain
The drivers cuss the winged hopes on their heels,
Hoping to get home for supper
Before something else ruins their day
Knowing that when he chooses he will choose
As he has chosen
As have they themselves
Finally, to dare no more than one dares
To live so that one will not be forgotten
Buying that bit of immortal stroking
Piece by piece, by smile or favor
By appropriate chastisement or unnotice,
Not knowing though that though his choice is set,
This time when he places his bet
He's dealing with a new measure of chance.
But he doesn't know it may be the last time

THE MARVELOUS LAND OF INDEFINITIONS

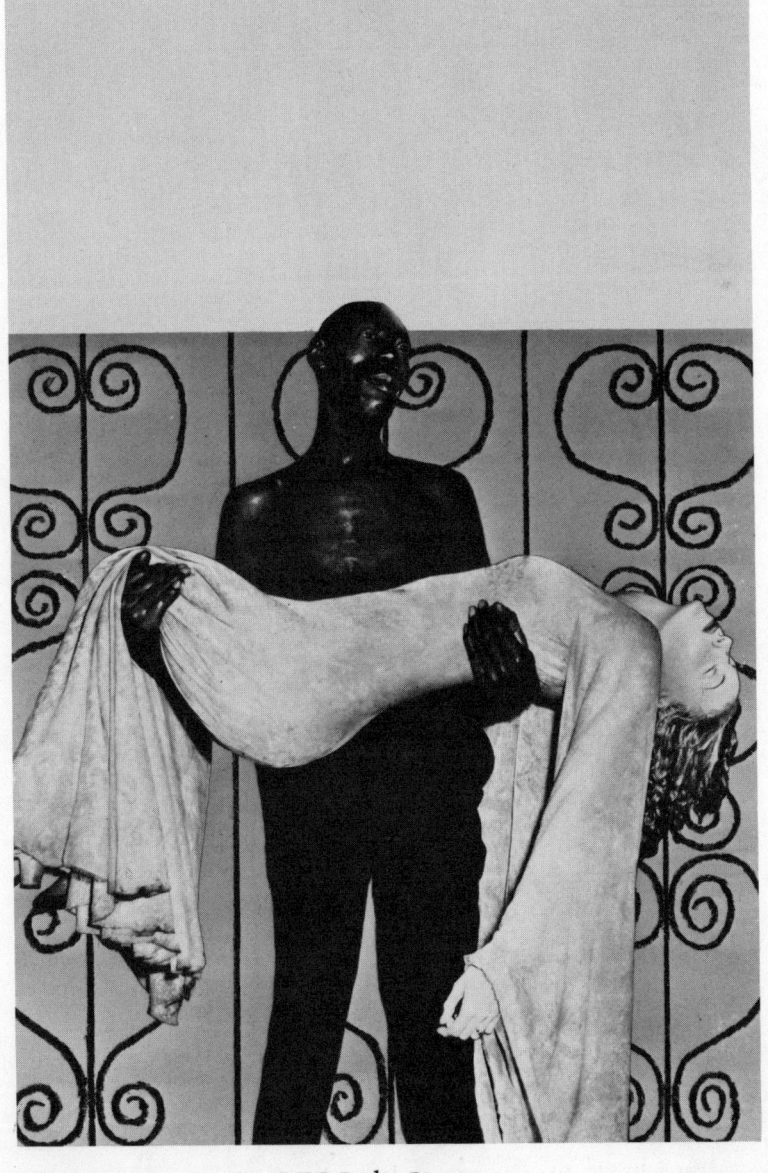

I Walked with a Zombie, RKO Radio Pictures, 1956, reprinted by permission.

"You know, life is just a puzzle...."
—*Roosevelt Sykes*

The Marvelous Land of Indefinitions
> The poet's business is telling the truth.
> —Ricardo Miro

How nice! How convenient!
We have all gathered to read & listen to poems
As if everyone were actually equal
Laborers in the corn fields
Girls in the cigarette factory
Though someone always seems to be saying
"A poet's task is making poetry . . . blah blah blah"

But poeting with poor people doesn't end poverty.

How sweet it is! How nice!
First poems and last words
Are heard here, dedicated to friends
Describing the ultimate artistic inspirations
Incorporating all the latest stops and turns
Of fashion

Example:
    the alleys oh like psychedelic birds
    & the transfiguration of being,
    of self, of the essence, blah blah blah
It's annoying.

Clearly, this poetry reading
Will not be heard in the town square
Because people don't listen to poetry
Since poetry is "the nectar of the gods"
And these readers are demigods

Raising up to nirvana and adulation
All of those others who read, write,
Or listen to this stuff

So
Tranquilly, everyone reads
After cocktails
    embraces

Happily, an interesting poem
Reminds me of Proust
Or something from a 16th Century French book
Afterward
No one assumes responsibility for sense or vision
Because, in the final analysis, poetry
Is something personal
        intimate
        alien

Newspaper headlines are full of lies
And the radio is full of lies
AND POETRY IS FULL OF LIES!

Because everyone goes along
In slavish style follows the ways of the world
(European, Anglo-Saxon, White)

And the *style,* the *form* is what's important
Incomprehensible to everyone else
But them. Oh, in the final analysis
Everyone else is a part of the problem
And we're in the "in" crowd.

The ones who never read are ready to gossip!

Did you see so & so's new book?
    I just got accepted in *Reader's Digest*
Blah blah blah

But that's OK
    OK because we made the best of it
Seated at god the father's right hand
OK because here where nothing's happening
No one can truthfully say
                    us least of all
That we're lazy
Hate to work,
Know nothing but gambling, drinking, *fiesta,* good sex
(the common definition of a Panamanian)
                            because
What's on our minds is the office,
                    security, the kids.
    Daily bread.
A payday every two weeks or the 30th

Everyone goes along
Because unemployment goes up every day
It's OK   exploit the farm workers
OK that rent keeps going up
OK
    that young people are lost in marijuana and "free love"
OK
    because all the world drinks Coca-Cola and smokes Viceroys
And everyone prefers blonds and white folks
And cathedral arched eyebrows
OK
    because the gringos don't worry themselves about anybody

(Only duck hunting in January—and that not too often—
And controlling the nation's economy)
OK
    because it's the others who suffer

In the final analysis, this is the 51st state
In the wonderful land of indefinitions
Where everyone goes along
Where poets gather to read poems
And sip cocktails
        And talk   har har har
        Chat   har har har blah blah blah
        Talk   har har har
To evade the compromise
Escape the moment
Avoid facing destiny and the "secret word"
        Each day growing clearer
        Each day   blah blah blah
        Hovering   blah blah blah
        Nearer

—*Roberto MacKay*

When Dukardo Boarded the Astro-Jet, He Already Done Seen the Movie
after Dukardo Hinestrosa

At an altitude of 9,000 feet
Above the simple level of my being
People seem all the same size
Whether Rockefeller or any child of Sanchez

Impossible to distinguish if they wear
Patent leather shoes or be completely naked.
If they have wisdom teeth still
Or gold fillings or go toothless

It's impossible to know if their faces
Are popular with beards or with lice
Or if the faces are regularly razored
With a Gillette, vehemently blue;

If they possess a lung of stainless steel
Or contact lenses. Or if the brain
Has been washed and dried in the sun
If their midriff has a plump Gordian knot
Or if the color of their toenails is enamelled
Lazily red

If on their heads now has begun
The interrupting drop
Of southern showers
Or the strokes of an epileptic hammer
Judiciously answering
The basal metabolism of each one.

At 9,000 feet in a jet
When the motors by reaction form
Millions of revolutions per second
It's impossible to know with certainty
Who suffers, below, from complexes
And who is freudianly infirm

It's impossible I suppose to suppose
If their fingertips are as clear
As water. If their fingerprints have been traced.

If, in spite of everything, the salt
Of their tears may be iodine

Or if their sex is compromised
With new birth-control pills
Promising to create no more beings
Destined for a radioactive mushroom

From 9,000 feet in the air on an Astro-Jet
It is natural:

Everything is very difficult to distinguish

Home X XI

Just come back from the zodico
Alone
Call my long-distance girl friend
Her boyfriend answers,
"Yeah? Lorenzo who?"

I come back to this place
But this place ain't mine.

Just come back from the zodico
Alone
Where your girl friend
Her boyfriend says oh yeah and who is you
Yeah

I just come back someplace
But this someplace ain't mine.

MMDCCXIII ½

The cruelty of ages past affects us now
Whoever it was who lived here lived a mean life
Each door has locks designed for keys unknown

Our living room was once somebody's home
Our bedroom, someone's only room
Our kitchen had a hasp upon its door.

Door to a kitchen?

And our lives are hasped and boundaried
Because of ancient locks and madnesses
Of slumlord greed and desperate privacies

Which one is madness? Depends on who you are.
We find we cannot stay, the both of us, in the same room
Dance, like electrons, out of each other's way.

The cruelties of ages past affect us now

An Excerpt from BIG HOUSE MOVIES

If any man were willing to change places, his ancestor would be a fool. In that one thought, the danger of the motion picture image reveals itself. Movie-watching is a Quixote's contest with the romance of non-being. It is an escape from the ego and the fears generated by the being of others.

Those others are the source of the ego's distractions, yet all of us are trained to rather not be ourselves. While fearing others. And what we fear in others is that they will interrupt the course of our own ambitions, or that they will support those ambitions and, in that way, hinder the accomplishment of our own disgust with ourselves.

Those sympathetically disposed to our success, especially that which has already been accomplished, might inspect their commitment before they are suspected of faint hearts.

Please pass the amyl nitrate.

One will appear quietly in the doorway, striped in the light from barred windows. A smile and a confessorial tone ensure no disassociation from decadent complicity in the world's varied violations of your threshold. The world is the others.

Every Big House movie has such a scene because that's what the TV set and the hugged-up drive-in folks want to see. The scene dramatizes what they believe to be the actual facts of their lives. A whispered word at the time-clock: "They're out to get you." A word from a wise guy is ordinarily sufficient to open the armory of paranoia's fleet mothball notions. . . .

Entire nations are being mothballed!

> *The doorway is the doorway to a closet*
> *and your skeleton is inside, caught in a holdup*

This scene is restricted, indeed, it is seldom actually shown on screen. It is the disturbing framework of the scenes that actually are screened. Ordinarily all of this is hidden in spoken narrative or dialogue of some sort, for we could not bear to watch it. No one wants to see the door closed, nor does anyone want the skeleton to break out (the Big House movies use the underworld argot "bust out") of its closet.

On another level, the entire rational spirit of nations mothballed in Christendom is viewed with fear and distrust. Yet all of that, too, is part of us. Which part is a game of "guesses, anybody" . . . just to keep the game going. But, for our own sakes, where the game is going should not be left up to guesswork.

Again, this is a dangerous psychological ledge . . . a case where "edge" is disadvantage. Say the secret word and then duck! After all, nobody likes a smart.

Samaritan! you cry to yourself. Suddenly, on the screen that monopolizes your sight, yourself multiplies into surly pickets. "Samaritan," you cry out in despair. And your other selves chant, "Pass 'm by!"

What are they all hepped up about? Something in the scenario that seems to escape you but, since you are paying attention, means something. And that something is threatening.

The problem of the mothballed nations. It touches the same psychological overload line. The very popular Zombie movies flirt with this reaction in the selves of the viewers. We are willing to put up with the antics of the walking dead because we are assured that they, in recompense for their post mortem mischief, will be reduced to dust at the end of the photograph. But in the case of *actual* entire mothballed nations we have no such assurance.

The Zombie and Big House movies represent only the tip of the iceberg. In their own way, the Jack Johnson and Iceberg movies touch on the nerve endings of the public psyche and batter us as if we were Titanics. We live our lives like ships that pass in the night.

Our stunted love blinks red and green, port and starboard, like an indecisive traffic light. Even our belated cries for help go out as redundant stutterings SOS SOS SOS like the redundancy of the motion picture frames fooling us into commiseration with the film's wraiths of light. And we love those phantoms of the Loew's, even as we fear human others. Andrea Dorias list in each one's imagination, in the oceans of their heads behind western eyes, a frighteningly real possible thing.

"Don't look now, but...."

Or the childish game that ends in embarrassment. Well, if you knew your fly was zippered why did you look down! Huh?

—The others laugh and look down.

You think, *I'm a fool to fear.* But the steel guitar does not come in behind you. No drums. No fiddle. You were right in the first place ... the agony starts all over again as the next scene fades into sight.

This is exactly the effect of going to the movies or cheaply watching last year's flops on TV. The scenarios are each of them elaborate versions of that kid stuff. Open fly.

Big finale: The car pulls up to the door of the mansion just in time, rustling the leaves in the drive. That's in the Upper Class movies. In the Big House movies, there is no such saving chase. You and your ego are left in the doorway, fearing the close of the door ... striped in the theatrical light from barred windows ... annoyed by a preacher and a screw.

Scream your guts out. No one will hear you. If they do, they will lean over and say *Shhhhhhhh, I'm trying to hear.*

But this is old stuff. What filmed personal disaster accomplishes in testing the individual psyche (ego, you & me against the world), the Disaster films perform on a yet coarser scale. In the Disaster movies the dangerous others are dehumanized and, in that sense, made entertaining. Just like electric dishwashers.

Nancy Pickett says that in Cathay they had a habit of burying servants when the mandarins died. In the same burial mound. As times changed, good help became hard to get. So they started making porcelain servants.

Nowadays we have dishwashers and egos. The egos are merely spiritual leaks that need washers. But we also have needs and human fears, and good help is so hard to find. So God invented the movies. These eyeball enemas flush the brain of any sensible concern.

Screen Test

> Don't count the time lost, neither. . . .
> —*Robert Browning*

Consider thoughts to live
In life
In golden coils,
Her spirit clasps you
Hugs you close
To learning life's considerations
Gamely flutter
Pennants panties
Scenes badly-lit
In old movies
On the sheet tacked up
On the wall
Off the wall
Jazz solos against space
Feeling the people's sigh
Or soft voice harmonies
Describing the origin of sighs:

A volcanic garden.
Dark-panelled walls
Dusty dim Tiffany lamps
Pictures of Burn-out Johnson
Shutting em down
At Daytona or Summernationals
Scoring a long-disputed TKO over
Underrated Kid Flash

The quiet Paddock Bar in New Orleans
The Tack Room in Hot Springs
Beneath Bold Ruler's fading portrait

Our booth
Embraced in privacy's dim recall

The gentle homing instincts of a life
Spent well and gently
In a world's turmoil: The green of sporting felt
Color television astroturf
Pointilliste lawns & formal gardens
All silence yearning

To operate the mind in three dimensions,
Smoke if you've got em
Sleep lightly in American accents
Sighs

Bartered like any other eloquence
Remembered, quoted

Prizes of some moment, far or recent
Shining in memory
Hollywood premiere searchlights
Scanning neon-blushing skies
For stars more brilliant
Than those whose limos birth them on the pavement
Impressed by the footprints of other earlier average
Americans who ascended in biograph light

Lips pout
Or catch the tongue between their fulsomeness
To seize her sighs
And still his questionings

Teeth flash and click,
Recover earlier imposter accents

A line vanishes
smudge
The words flee into telephonic moments
The silent poses that accompany the voice
Across charged ethers grown heavy with manners
And distance's natural doubts

Echoes of our accents fortify us
Against these moments when the posse betrays
Us only to ourselves
The foot put right the proper laugh
Imposter phone booth shush a pirate haven

All our theatrics spring from private laws
Losses and moments, the first time seeing ourselves

Wrongly, a line vanishes
In a split second's prodigalness
Receiver cocked to the wrong ear
An inappropriate surmise of levity
His awkward charm
The others' puzzling elaborations

First, the pose. Then the posse

A self-portrait would have it
Oh him

Though others shall continue their puzzles of faith
Faithless wit, agonizing self-eradications
Awkward charm and flea market momentous worries
"Ladybug, ladybug . . ." Such things happen.

Occurrences fill the morning radio like kisses
Or the working man's stale-mouthed recriminations
For example,
There's the show in the phone booth
The numbers quickly scratched on the wall
Desperate labanotations
An awkward pas forging ahead despite of
Interruptions

In woodlands, forests, open spaces
Now
We primp ourselves on country odors
Denim cigaret smoke breath of beer
Lite
Sunlit dust and shadowed forest streaming
Through the weft of garments and hair
And sunlit dust of pose around the phone
Speaking to distances in person

And, naturally, the distant ones in person
Have to be doing just the same to reconcile us
To the terror of our personal space. Space
Filling with all the dreams we decipher from logic
And late conversation

Recollection of the pose in the booth
Teddy Nadler, Eichmann, lover at the headache plateau
Reflection of the dance in the gloss of the glass
Facing the speaker with angles of traffic
And the breeze blowing through the smashed pane

This space missing the pane we take for granted
Taking this light show of our concern's affection

Granted, it's a moment's escape. A spectacle
Of awe for one's own attachments

Unwilling grace

Stubborn blessings dog the beaten heart
Like obnoxious but useful reporters
Tripping over microphone cords,
Stumbling in Charles Laughton's profound footprints

Retiring into the light

All of the all of the all of the feeling, bold
Reduced to a mismanageable ease
A cartoon. 20th Century Fox logo footage
Universal's glass world,
Daring Wiley Post aeroplane
Circling a world premature record
Amelia Earhart disappearing curtsy women's lip
Introducing performance
Of disguised boredom and banality
Blaaaah! And classic violin concerto
Classic horrors (plucked from grave,
Collaged from charnel house, the living
Dead)

Footprints handprints dentured kisses in the stone
Ghoulish commonplaces of celebrity
Glees manufactured not to be forgotten

& other commonplaces:
Dancing dots
Kyle's Egyptian block in Beaumont, Texas
Modern art nouveau

Yes, why does popular America persist in death dreams?
Kyle's in Beaumont. Modern times, King Tut?

Paramount's cartoon McKinley soaring
Bound with stars
Above the motion picture beneath it
"All they show these days," says Duke, "is garbage"
Purposeful poses of the seeking lost
Childish posses
Kindly portraits of urbane Josephites

Columbia's animated Aphrodite
Luciferous gem of the ocean
Twinkling in comic-strip butterfly light
Stolen from dreams to illumine
Dull turns of mannered script

The cursive swirl and curl of RKO Radio music
Different so in these days of motivation
As if sounds were not memories also,
As if motivations are not remembered old tunes
"The story unfolds . . ."
Pictures of pictures in disciplined tone range
Xerox
Black & white

Consider, girl, these images to live
In life
In golden coils,
In thoughts recovered
Hip postures of faded stagings
4,000 whisperings in darkened halls,
"*King Lear,* Act 1, sc. iii"
To stay the guilt of trashy tabloids

Wrinkled ephemerides
Which feature every star's comings
And goings on

Can I mention "Round Midnight" here
As she reads me the Bible? I will
Probably consent in the morning, seeking a word
The word one word to remember
And the posings just shuffle along
Congregations, medleys of ancient hit tunes
Into and out of your mind

Consider life itself to be a puzzle
Like a highway as it appears on a map

Consider you yourself lost in a delta
Of a sudden river you did not expect
Did not expect this woman did not anticipate
The toilsome burdens of a simple space
Touching her hand, romantically feeling shy
When shy you've never been in all remembrance

Be careful how you touch her
She may awaken . . .
Within her dreams it seems to him he's something special
Oh him
Before she awakens to make up her mind,
Before she hides her face in her dream,

A fear exists that's packaged in illusion
Like seeds in their packets
Like verses of a song heard somewhere
Considered in a particular pastime moment
With her or without her
All of it coming clearly to mind

Her life and his exemplified in golden coils
Cardioid warmth, images and music
Attending pose each pose and change of mind
Your fascination stepped-up and refined
Modulated by the flickering changes of light
As the movie goes from the drawing room
To the chaise everyone's been talking about
Soft, loving light in the close-up
The first time you kiss her. The chase ends.
The movie ends. Headlights go on like candles
As the tornado looms in the screen door
Her head on his shoulder, sleeping prettily
Softly, as he drives home
Singing catches of the hits on the radio
Lost in the Beatles, seeing her pretty
Strayed and exiled in the changes of some insinuating blues
Seeing the headlights pass in curls around her hair
Studied in affection's sidelong glances
Now & then. At any other time, hands on the wheel!
Eyes firmly on the road!

Like our poor memories of Hot Springs afternoons,
The loving conversations as other bettors wailed,
The blues pulse out their crude approximations
Somber, in kinks of words we barely hear to understand
We only recognize familiar turns of music

She'd cry if she was wakened
Or is it you the only one who'd weep
For her awakening
Tears for your own déshabillage of esteem's emotions
And guilt to woo the weeping

The lie confirms
The strongest instinct is to beg the question
Oh him and beg it further
My luck damn sure is looking up
These days, it smiles and cares
In nearness now beside me, in my hand
Even the distance wishes fortune & a smile

Illusion stops
Stock still
It stopped stuck
Like a tv football game in instant replay
A mighty wave of joy
A zzzing radio zzzzzzz
Pretty cheerleader in a cowboy hat
Arched in a japanese woodblock
Hiroshige moment
Stolen frozen Chosen

And oh! if she awakened
Oh what sorrow!

To see too much in a moment of him
Overseen like First National's lot
Acres of quonset huts and block buildings
Where passably creative magic churns
To fill dull weekends at the country drive-ins
With schemes and joy and terrors of teen hearts
Vaguely intent on these plottings

Hung here in space extravagant wallpaper
Willingly mutable to squeeze a smile,
A happy reminiscence, sense of portent,
Laughter, homely yearning, adrenal rushes

Oh him (this time a mystery movie), *some* delicious response
From those who are preoccupied with yearning!

Kaleidoscopic tear?

Consider, then, in life,
In golden coils of daily expectation
The certain fear persists
That she may wake and weep
That slightly parted sleeping lips
Will speak and name you clearly

Joyful nods and elbow prods of recognition
Sweep your fandom.

God

You can either sit facing the jukebox
Standing in interminable popcorn lines
Missing the credits
Facing the future soundless on the other screen
A tabloid smile for the birdie
The photograph that will eventually appear
"In Happier Days" if you want to,

You can appeal to a guarded fanatic within you
Bleating "amen" in a pleasure, like a child's
Indefinable and beyond transcription
Except a buoyant quality of warmth
In a climate growing dark with indecision
Where skies are white as envelopes
And the Liberty Bell on the stamp floats like an airship
Bearing dreams, snapshots, and loneliness complaints

Tears and heats of absence grows this fear

The harvest clutters every drawer and cranny
With glimpsed impediments
Half-served considerations
Faces and hours curled on the cutting room floor,
To be nostalgic and romantic about it—
Priceless bebop 78s she scratched beyond repair
Giggling. Or clumsily sat on.

Or you can go create yourself
Great power and joy in your exiles
Contemplating "Three Years of Torture"
Percy Mayfield's murky bayou of a voice
Spilling into all around and through the house
Through perennial cardboard cones
Reminding you of pinetrees and magnolias
Smiling, waving as the flashbulbs awaken
Adroitly graceful, gliding around Alan Ladd's
And Mickey Rooney's elevator shoeprints
Barely, acknowledging the screaming throng's flirtations
Secure in the coils of her love and her distance,
Her head resting on your shoulder. And you, poised,
On the threshold of cleverer interpretations.

Class Action

One person amplified one hundred
Thousand times
Assumes that he
Or she must be, at least, wallpaper
As important as that

(At least) as being on the radio calling the jock
Dedicating on the air one temporary tune
Composed by amateurs and marketed by pros
To Junior and Susie, Diana with her fine self
JT and Bobo, P.P. and Poppa, Willie Rae,
That tired old Delois
                  watch yourself now brother man
Hey
    sweet sweet Sally,
From the little bitty one to Mister Heartbreaker
Two Ten-Four and Wild Turkey
They know who they are
                  heh heh
The "Astoria Queens"
                yeah

Who do you   wa tch tch now, watch it!
    think
Who do you think would send this out to you
                              yeah
LT from South Park
            check it out, baby
Sending it all out
        for you

Sending it
        all   sending this one out for the Sunnyside children
Beautiful Lady Jo, with her bad self
                              oh yeah
Margaret Anne, Rapunzel & all the guys
                             down
To the Possessive Tower Physical Fitness Center
                                    yeah
All
Who have chosen this particular hit to justify our time
Spent dancing to it, and clarify the meaning of our times

A
Three or four hundred years
Go whistling by
The graveyards of perception
Like in a 1930s movie,
Self-serving histories of the self-serving
What really killed Vaudeville

Calendars flipping crazily, newspaper headlines
Twirling into the sidewalk's sudden view,
The blind man in the kiosk groping toward the NEWS
Was the wallpaper, shrunk-sided
Art Deco filling the movie houses of the plains
Venetian palaces in potato-land
Putting all the blacks in the loft
Keeping them in segregated places
Above the ushers stationed by the stairs
To herd them ever upward

That the orchestra escape infection of the Blues
Red-suited ushers guided us aloft

While white Americans below were entertained
By wraiths of aberration on the screen
All black & white to them, all hats and horses;
To us, variations of blues, as the light rose
And churned in the vault of the house and cigar smoke
Swirling toward our ordained roost

Balcony wallflower seats
Formerly reserved for the nobles
In the days they were still sane
In Europe

We spat on the groundlings from there
From our balcony quarters
Which made Genet call us niggers
Jujubes rained down to the floor
Matting the cornsilk heads of Doom's scions

We chewed the Jujubes before we hurled them

In Africa, the spirits pout
For stardom on the silver screen

    Silver has blue in it, plus black and white
And passes for one thing and another
                               if you spend it right

    We are the wallpaper fraying
Out of woodwork anchors
We are asking questions and question answers
Too vague to be forgotten for their haste

There is really nothing to get all upset about

Nothing chronic answers a child's curses

Nobody gives a damn what niggers say
Calypso songs are spoofed & pooh-poohed every day.
In Africa, the spirits pout;
The militants think they'll win
Without a doubt, there is something going on
But really nothing to get hot about

Proverbs are lozenges in dusty peach
Prophecies swirl in borders near the floor

We are the wallpaper.

Scrolling outward, withered in the heat of answers
Formed in hate and haste
And all the waste of time on aberration
Considered "entertainment" in our time

While spirits pout, we others spot and fade
Spinning with fortune like unspooling film
Unleashing great comedians and pissed-off heroes,
Doomed ingenues expiring without perspiring
In molten gardens filled with sighs and silent
Movie glances

That's entertainment
                       the force of circumstance
Is stronger than one thinks
It draws on everything and riddles hope
Circles the future on our calendars
Claims all the past its own
                       as memory's "I told you so"
As indiscriminate as vacuums clutching air

Each vision (even simple sight, foresight,
I told you so) is what is sheltered from this force

Which wouldn't necessarily harm it
The way air unthinkingly crushes its absence
To entertain the kids in Physics I
Circumstance would rather surround it
An invisible shield
A force field of a 1930s fantasy.
Vision would shrink from lack of danger
A tunnel of hot security and boredom
A searing light cylinder of lens projection
Saved from the clumsiness of needed dreamers

That's life
        motion pictures you've seen and forgotten
The plot or the message
                even the stars

Only continuity remains
Attention that abides within each moment
Filed in recollection
Opens in repose, touching the flesh
With actual motion
Fingertips glow slightly, lips and eyes
Juggle flickering smiles and heavy sighs

Like wallpaper, America designs
Ourselves
Projections in the dark
Children of genius whose inventions
Include the ferris wheel,
Passing the buck,
The choking sky, a genealogy
Stolen to wanting mothers
Who disguise each fear as love, each want as discipline

Sometimes in anger
Bright with this heritage, we push
Our minds father logical jazz

What shall I do but speak
In Africa, the juju spirits shout through us
Our screams speak rapture of their presence,
Not our pain (which is unutterable).
Without them, we would live in silent movies
Which now bereft of Orpheums or Hippodromes,
Apollos or Bijous, would have us acting out our lives
In Five Oaks 6s, Midtown Twins,
And anagrams of corporate collusion

In Africa, the spirits gad about like niggers
Long, shiny shone shoes! Amazing limousines
With music blasting speeding to heaven and back
On superhighways carved from inspired trees!
And that ain't nothing

If I should speak, the wallpaper would break
Its silence, too.
Should I despite some fiction of myself
To talk, as the wallpaper should?
Should I forget myself because spirits are talking
Or pleas to you or yourself or your master
When, obviously, no plea does no good
And any plea at all does little better
Than simply being there, like the woodwork;
Working yourself up like wallpaper.

Hurling Jujubes down on their heads,
The ones who fear the Blues unless they're silvered,
In the darkened theater

Does as little good as the pleasure of being ignored
Being stolen away from yourself
One casual phrase at a time, or suddenly
A traumatic abduction from your own projection
Anxious yes and easeful as your "òwn"
Or after slackening of care by days
Being looked at as if you were wallpaper;
As strategy, it isn't logical a bit
But if it works, it's a breakthrough to logic.

Unlettered negroes called this logic Jazz
Relating thought to life, love to projection
Spirit entertained by spirit
                       as in life
And when the movies chose to speak
                                the voice was Jazz
Projected through the fantasy of aberration
For which the blame accrues to those who thought
That anyone was free to choose among spirits
Like segregating folks
                    or seating suckers at the picture show.
The logic holds its own
                    configuration

Patterns of light of thought of sound must move
Patterns are meant to bounce away
From walls; the ones that stick there . . . .
Kente cloth moves when woman works
                             to praise the weaver
While flattery and hate speak without guile
                               to the believer
A hunter sharpening his knife
Is honing eyes to flesh the spirit

From the tree into his life; and
The musician, cranking keys and twining strings
Imagines he can hold his voice inside his hand

These things are true, told beautifully
They sometimes teach us to sleep, to learn there
That truth is beautiful while we are sleeping.
We are entertained by turns of logic
Flickering upon us with a grain of sense
Strained carefully from daylight, like a dream.
But rudely told, the truth just spreads.
Discretion lost, it multiplies its faces
Shimmering
Like a voice understood pealing outward
Ringing and extending its reach
Preening its facets to make echoes jealous

If no one speaks, the truth will still
Be true. Poor thing, unspoken.
False friends snickering behind
Her back, echoes piping up
With snide conceits
All about English lakes and valleys wild
Paul Whiteman's greatness & all that jazz

In Africa, the spirits kiss their teeth

Wallpaper oh?

The second power of arithmetic is grammar
Disguised as laws, as favors, getting over
Getting it together, getting straight
Just for a minute getting straight for what it feels like
Keeps you poor. That's what it feels like.
Feeling poorly

For just a minute, put a sad smile on your face
The badge of honored membership in the inhuman race
Toward contortions of emotion known as Art
When other people spend the money. Considered
Guile and in cahoots when you're important.

    Ain't it the truth?

You're blessed.
You don't have to decide which which is which
Just got to feel it
Don't have to give a damn
If you don't care,
Someone will explain what you would say
If there was anything you could say
After all your vast experience against the wall

Fading there, drawn on
                        ripped-off
Finally, if you won't speak
                        dream
That student radicals will
Provide a new generation of protest
Crazy posters upon your foundation
That happy families or anarchist avant-gardes
Will superimpose their slides and films
On your strong patterns
                        A waste of space
Disguised as privacy, as thoughts, as getting even
Show them all
            yeah

You've got strong backing
                        yeah

But it's up against
                the wall

You're getting flakey.

                Behold the spirits,
With their lips poked out,
They look just like the people in the street
Who wind in patterns of elated doubt
And depressing certainties
That send them jogging circles around life
Just like the movie people reel around
Sane conversations in real restaurants
And their own private swimming pools,
Trapped in the truthless patterns of the light
That entertains us in the darkness of our lives
Where papered walls compete with littered streets
For eloquence

We succumb to all mythologies of moments
All so subtly disguised as loss of care
Liquids that turn to film and film to powder
Tripping, getting off
Up till our lives are filled with minuses
Or finally we cling to one alone,
Everything is true but us about us.

And I'm a lie! Because I see in twos or threes,
Because my view is amplified by night
Crazily flies into the dawning sun
Cussing & fussing like it supposed to bes
A natural man

Because my spirit slaps me upside my head
And makes me turn to see the others pouting
Because by lack of eloquence
I'm left here to embarrass you by shouting
That we must speak or be like patterns on a wall,
Moving or pasted still, it doesn't matter which

    You don't have to take my word
For "it"

Hat Red

The earth remains the kind of saucer Sally saw in the decadent gardens of the upper East side on the night of the day of the great blackout.

Remember the silly Rosh Hashonna on the 17th floor? The sillier Yom Kippur in Evanston noticing for the first time the horns on the roof of the Illinois Central station? That's why Monk has got to wear that silly pork pie hat.

The UFOs hung calmly in the velvet pitch above the dimmed skyline, their radios monitoring unintelligible broadcasts of Lyndon Johnson's unintelligible Texas drawl. Lyndon was wringing his hands. Lindsley was wringing Mike Quill's bull neck *in absentia*. Somehow the TWU was behind it, he knew it. But somehow they were not the culprits this time.

Dim-lit cabarets got mucho dimmer. The combos played the sinking liner songs. "Good-bye Dodge Boy Hat" segue "Be it ever so humble . . . there's no place like home." "Clark in the Dark." All by ear. Damn sure couldn't read no music. Huh!

From the rim of the saucer, the terrain dipped gracefully toward a silken palisade across the Hudson. It could be seen as a darker, shiny black against the black. And somewhere eons away a burn-off stack at an Esso plant in Camden flickered in the blackness like a red feather in a Harlem cowboy hat. 50s version. A smooth curving blackness was the earth's jealousy of the sky's vault that poets and artists had been prating about since the days of Michael Angelo, one of their capos.

Beep buboop! Beep beep bubop! You know how they invented all those words.

I know this is all true because I woke up on the F train at the last stop 179th St after falling asleep on my way home from work, the hard work and the downers did that. And when I woke up, all the lights were off and the train was deserted and I remembered Baraka's *Dutchman* and got scared and thought O shit can this be some kind of a joke or is this the end or is this the end of the line or the last stop again or the world hunh. Some of these questions went through my ha ha mind. And in the street on top of the station confusion was literally raining or reigning. The only lights were the headlights. And my head had gone out! The busses were full of smirking people the bastards while the subway riders did Chicken Little bits on the sidewalk. Their heads had done gone out.

My feet lightly touched on the ground.

Two young girls walked down 169th St bearing candles giggling saying "Pilgrim, blessings upon thee" as I ran into Triboro Records to see if the music was going if Ric thought this trip could be real. Ric said, Hey man, can you dig this? So I figured something had to be usual, even if I was still in the dark. What the hell.

Who is this fool in the comic cosmic zootsuit gaucho slouch brim hat? The only light the glistening pearl in his hatband. And shouldn't there be a light in the window?

At home, the folks were listening to emergency WNEW radio dumb show broadcasts kerosene generator-style just like way off back in the country or Nha Be, Viet-Nam detailing how Lyndon was in Washington DC the comparatively City of Light at the moment, wringing his hands. Wondering how he could get the Air Force into JFK Int'l Airport to keep orders lessen the Viet Kongs snuk in under covers of darkness (just they style) and do some strange number while the streetlights was dozing and the nigger catchers (strontium light) slept in the UFO darkness of a sudden technological Cimmeria at the edge of the earth. But goddammit in New York City?

Hush your mouf! That's Nixon style. Get back, Baudelaire! It was getting to getting that deep. The peoples was frantic and suddenly very uncool. De dark ages.

Sun Ra considered the whole thing amusing. For several weeks after all the lights went on again, he smiled as if to say I told you so and kept showing us a clipping from the *National Enquirer* that purported to show flying saucers hovering all over the city. It was to die! Skeptics insisted it was no flying saucers but glare on the photographer's lens. Glare from where?

We sure felt dumb. Sitting there in the dark looking stupidly into the glistening of each other's eyes. That is, if you were smart enough to have a candle.

"Don't just stand there looking like a wet dream, do something!" And "what the hell you want *me* to do! Do I look like goddam Con Ed to you?" Brother against brother. And so on. Although, even in the light of all that, the light stayed Off.

And it wasn't until the next several hours, after the devil smiled and tipped his Hatlo hat, and the shine from the bald head underneath the black crown turned up the sunlight like an Ace in a tight moment at the table when all your goddamm money's all most gone, you know. Yes, it was just the smile of the other side of the hat.

The heat was off. And inside the enigma was shiny silk lining turning silly silk nuance colors in the light and gold well "gold" anyway initials monogrammed on the sweatband. A distinct change. And thank goodness gracious. The hat, in the sudden natural daylight, was shaped like a cardinal's hat (the black one they wear in the daytime, not the red one for the holy parade). Nevertheless. Sometimes even now all these years later, off downs and sober except for the six-pack of Falstaff, I shudder to think.

What if he'd been wearing the red hat, the one with the cute little tucks and points on the sides . . . the cardinal points . . . how would *that* have gone down?

Gentile Horus!

It's a lucky thing we're so lucky. It's like we have to keep on making errors and having the cosmos surprise us. But we always seems to be able to lick it. Even if it means stick sticking it out (whatever the sticky situation) till the sunrise. Or any old other natural same old Egyptian so-called Roman thing.

Owhhh!

I'm so breathless because this is too true. And it's still true today. It did happen for true and I saw it. Or did not see it, that is, I mean in the darkness. And there is a many true words in this story of that day that *was* a night in New York City. Some of the holy ones are articles and verbs nouns and so forth. It was a sign from greater powers than we be and, so sadly, few of we on earth have heed the signals hidden there and then in that dark.

I don't know about no UFO, but I do know Anne weeps for all sentient beings. And I know my brother Ishmael cusses. I'm too mean for either of that. But I tell you, it's a goddamm lucky thing we're so lucky.

Clear Channel

Ha ha. You searching
For money
Find affection.
An object found

Touched by that one's hand

Kirlian fetish

This is supposed to go on
Without interruption
Until something surprising
Emerges or surfaces and

Contemplates the reversal:

For an instant
Teardrops and raindrops
Ascend like fountains,

Then back to gravity cliches

It's all your fault, Edgerton!